More Redneck Jokes

by

Jim Bob Buford
and
"Shotgun" Jack Grabowski

**BARNES
&NOBLE
BOOKS**
NEW YORK

ISBN 0-7607-0881-9

Cover cartoon by John Caldwell
Cartoons on pp. 39 and 61 are copyrighted by *The New Yorker
Magazine*, Inc.

Text design by Noble Desktop Publishers

Printed and bound in the United States of America

98 99 00 01 02 M 9 8 7 6 5 4 3 2 1

This book is dedicated to Barbara, my wife and my sister, as well as my Ma and Pa, my Uncle Lester and my Aunt Lenore, my three cousins, my brothers Richard, Bob, and Richard Junior, and my Grandma Harriet and my Great Uncle Big Richard. If I've overlooked anyone else who lives in my trailer, I'm real sorry.

—Jim Bob Buford

Me too.

—Jack Grabowski

A man in Georgia, out for an afternoon of skydiving, jumped from an airplane while at 10,000 feet. When he pulled his parachute cord, however, it broke. As he plunged toward the ground and certain death, he saw a man below him rising rapidly into the air. As their paths crossed, one falling towards the earth and the other rising away from it, the skydiver yelled, "Excuse me! You wouldn't happen to know anything about parachutes, would you?"

"Sorry, I don't," the other yelled back. "Would you happen to know anything about lighting gas stoves?"

A ventriloquist was working in the deep south when a redneck suddenly stood up during his act and yelled, "Hey, you! You been making smart-ass remarks about us southerners being stupid all night long! We're not all stupid, ya know!"

"Relax," replied the ventriloquist, "they're just harmless jokes!"

"I'm not talking to you, pal!" answered the redneck. "I'm talking to that little jerk sitting on your knee!"

Billy Ray called the hospital in a panic. "You gotta send help!" he yelled. "My wife's going into labor!"

"Calm down," said the nurse. "Is this her first child?"

"No!" replied Billy Ray. "This is her husband!"

Scooter and Willie Fred were driving down the road in their pickup truck when a rabbit suddenly ran across the road right in front of them. Scooter slammed on the brakes, but not in time. He hit the rabbit, who went flying through the air before coming to earth in a heap. Willie Fred leaped from the car, picked up the rabbit, and cried out, "Scooter! We can't let him die like this! Quick, do something!"

"Wait right there," said Scooter. "I have something in the back that might help."

Scooter ran around to the back of the truck and returned with an aerosol spray can. "Hold up the rabbit," he instructed Willie Fred.

Willie Fred held up the injured bunny while Scooter sprayed him with the mist from the can. The rabbit immediately lifted up his head and looked around. He jumped out of Willie Fred's hands and began hopping down the road. After going about ten yards, he turned around, waved at the two men, and continued hopping. After going another ten yards, he again turned around and waved, then continued on his way. He repeated this over and over until he disappeared from sight.

"That's amazing," exclaimed Willie Fred. "What was in that can you sprayed him with?"

Scooter looked at the can. "Permanent Wave for Damaged Hare," he read.

Q: How do you confuse a redneck?

A: Put him in a round room and tell him to sit in the corner.

Bo and Jesse were talking while Bo was milking his cow. Suddenly, a fly zoomed right into the cow's ear. The cow started jumping around violently, shaking its head and mooing loudly. Bo tried to steady the cow, but just as suddenly, it settled down all by itself. Jesse looked down and noticed the fly was in the milk pail.

"Gee," said Jesse. "How'd that fly get down there so fast?"

"Easy," mused Bo. "In one ear, out the udder."

Young Roy Dale was crossing a road one day when a frog called out to him and said, "If you kiss me, I'll turn into a beautiful princess."

The young redneck bent over, picked up the frog, and put it in his pocket. Again the frog spoke out, "If you kiss me and turn me back into a beautiful princess, I will stay with you for one whole year."

Roy Dale took the frog out of his pocket, smiled at it, and once again returned it to his pocket. The frog cried out, "If you kiss me and turn me back into a princess, I'll stay with you for a year, and do anything you want."

Again the southern lad took the frog out, looked at it, and put it back into his pocket yet again. Finally, in frustration, the frog asked, "What's the matter? I've told you I'm a beautiful princess, that I'll stay with you for a year, and that I'll do anything you want. Why won't you kiss me?"

Smiling at the frog, Roy Dale said, "Look, I'm a redneck. I don't have time for a girlfriend. But a talking frog is cool."

Q: Why don't rednecks become politicians?

A: They're overqualified.

The Pope was on a rare trip to the United States. While traveling through the south, he was riding in a specially made sporty Popemobile provided for him by the President. The Pope begged the chauffeur to let him drive. Finally, the chauffeur gave in and let the Pope get behind the wheel. Naturally, the Pope went a little crazy and began going too fast. Eventually, he ran a stop light and was pulled over by a redneck policeman. The cop called his station to ask them what to do because he just pulled over somebody very, very important.

"Who is it?" asked his sergeant. "The mayor, a movie star?"

"Well, I'm not really sure," replied the cop, "but he must be a VIP. The Pope is his chauffeur!"

Three redneck construction workers were on a building site down south eating their lunch. Sam Earl opened his lunch box and exclaimed, "I don't believe it—a tuna fish sandwich again! If I get another tuna fish sandwich tomorrow, I'm going to climb up the scaffolding and jump off!"

Homer opened his lunch box and exclaimed, "Can you believe it? A cheese sandwich again! If I get another cheese sandwich tomorrow, I'm going to climb up the scaffolding and jump off!"

Cooter opened his lunch box and exclaimed, "Oh, no! A ham sandwich again! If I get another ham sandwich tomorrow, I'm going to climb up the scaffolding and jump off too!"

The next day came, and they all sat down to lunch. Sam Earl opened his lunch box. "I don't believe it!" he cried. "Tuna!" He climbed up the scaffolding and jumped to his death.

Homer opened his lunch next. "Oh, no!" he screamed. "Cheese!" He, too, climbed up the scaffolding and plunged to the ground far below.

Cooter finally opened his lunch box. "Oh, no!" he yelled. "Ham!" Cooter also climbed up the scaffolding and plummeted to his death.

The following week, the funeral for the three friends took place. The neighborhood priest, Father Murphy, walked around, comforting the widows. Sam Earl's widow, weeping, said to him, "I don't understand it. If only he had told me, I would have given him something different!"

Father Murphy approached Homer's widow. "I don't understand it either," she cried. "If he had only told me, I would have packed him something different!."

Finally, the priest made his way to Cooter's widow, who was bawling madly. "I *really* don't understand it," she exclaimed. "Cooter always made his own sandwiches!"

Young J.T. was bragging to his friends at school about his knowledge of the state capitals. "Go ahead," he said proudly. "Ask me any one. I know them all."

"Okay," said Clyde. "What's the capital of Wisconsin?"

"That's easy," replied J.T. "W."

While on a trip to the big city, Billy George walked up to a woman on the street and said, "Excuse me, ma'am. Do you know what time it is?"

"Why, yes, it's 3:15," replied the woman.

"You know," said Billy George, "it's the weirdest thing. I've been asking that question all day long, and each time I get a different answer."

Doodle tried to get into the local dance club, but they wouldn't let him in because he wasn't wearing a tie. Ticked off, he went back to his pickup truck, tied jumper cables around his neck, and approached the club again.

"Okay," said the bouncer. "You can come in—but don't start anything."

"Here's a song I wrote myself. It's called 'You Done Something To My Heart That I Can't Fix With Duct Tape.'"

Elroy had no faith in doctors, but when no other treatment seemed to help his aching back, he decided to see a chiropractor about it. Before his first appointment, he told the chiropractor of his reservations, but after a few adjustments, he felt better than he had in years.

"What do you think now?" the chiropractor asked.

"Well," replied Elroy, "I guess I stand corrected."

Bubba walked into work one day with both of his ears all bandaged up.

"What happened to your ears?" asked his boss.

"It's kind of embarrassing," said Bubba. "Yesterday I was ironing my shirt when the telephone rang. Danged if I didn't accidentally pick up and answer the iron."

"Okay," said his boss, "that explains one ear, but what happened to your other ear?"

"Well, jeez," explained Bubba, "I had to call the doctor, didn't I?"

Q: What do you do if a redneck throws a pin at you?

A: Run like the dickens—he's still got a hand grenade between his teeth.

Celebrating his new raise, a young lawyer went out and bought himself a brand-new red 1998 Ferrari. One of the most expensive cars in the world, it cost him over $200,000. He took it out for a spin and, while doing so, stopped for a red light. An old redneck on a moped, both looking about ninety years old, pulled up next to him.

The old man looked over the sleek, shiny new car and asked, "What kind of car ya got there, Sonny?"

"A 1998 Ferrari," bragged the lawyer. "It cost more than $200,000."

"That's a lotta money for a car," said the old man. "Why does it cost so much?"

"Because this car can do up to 200 miles an hour," boasted the proud young attorney.

"Can I take a look inside?" asked the old redneck.

"Sure," replied the owner.

The old man poked his head in the window and looked around. Leaning back on his moped, he said, "That's a right pretty car, all right!"

Just then the light changed. The lawyer decided to show the old man what his car could do. He

floored it, and within thirty seconds, the speedometer registered 200 miles per hour. Suddenly, the counselor noticed a dot in his rear-view mirror. It seemed to be getting closer and closer.

Whhhoooooooooosssssshhhhhh! Something shot by him, going twice as fast!

The lawyer watched in amazement and wondered, "What in the world could be going faster than my Ferrari?"

Suddenly, up ahead of him, he saw a dot coming toward him.

Whoooooooooooosh! Something streaked by him again! He got a quick glance, and it almost looked like the old man on the moped!

"Can't be," said the lawyer. "How can an old man on a moped outrun a Ferrari?" Suddenly, a dot again appeared in his rear-view mirror.

Whoooooooshhhhhhhh . . . Ka-BaMMMMM! Whatever it was plowed into the back of his car, demolishing the rear end.

The guy jumped out and, sure enough, it was the old man! The moped and the old geezer were lying in a pile. The guy ran up to the dying old redneck and said, "You're hurt bad! Is there anything I can do for you?"

"Yeah," replied the old redneck. "Unhook my suspenders from the side-view mirror on your car!"

A redneck's dilemma: Your dog's barking at the back door. Your wife's barking at the front door. Who do you let in? It's your call . . . but the dog'll stop barking when you let him in.

Duke decided he wanted to learn how to skydive. He went to an instructor and began taking lessons. On his first trip up in the plane, the instructor told Duke to jump out of the plane and pull his ripcord. The instructor explained that he would jump out right behind him so they would go down together.

As the time for the jump approached, the instructor again reminded Duke that he would be right behind him. Duke proceeded to jump from the plane. After free-falling for a few seconds, he pulled the ripcord and his chute opened. The instructor followed Duke out of the plane and pulled his ripcord, but his parachute did not open. Frantically trying to get his parachute open, the instructor flew past the redneck. Seeing this, Duke undid the straps to his parachute and yelled, "So you wanna race, huh?"

YOU KNOW YOU'RE A REDNECK IF...

. . . your wife has a spit cup on the ironing board.

. . . you think a good time is a bug zapper and a six-pack.

. . . people keep coming to your house thinking you're having a yard sale.

. . . you've been divorced and remarried three times and you still have the same in-laws.

. . . you refer to fifth grade as "my senior year."

. . . you can't marry your sweetheart because there are laws against it.

Jimmy Bob and Luke were working together building a house. Luke was putting up the siding. He picked up a nail, looked at it, and hammered it in. He picked up another nail, looked at it, and threw it away. He picked up another nail, looked at it, and hammered it in. He picked up the next nail, looked at it, and threw it away. This went on for quite a while. Finally, Jimmy Bob came over and asked him why he was throwing half of the nails away.

"Those ones were pointed on the wrong end," explained Luke.

"You idiot," replied Jimmy Bob. "Those are for the other side of the house!"

Scooter and Junior landed themselves jobs at a local sawmill. In the middle of the morning on their first day on the job, Scooter yelled out, "Junior! I lost my finger!"

"You lost your finger?" asked Junior. "How'd you do that?"

Scooter replied, "I just touched this big spinning thing here like thi. . . Damn! There goes another one!"

Louie Ray's wife telephoned him. "I think there's water in the carburetor," she said.

"Where's the car?" asked Louie Ray.

"At the bottom of the lake," she replied.

Cleevis was walking down the road, carrying a brown paper bag with him. He ran into Jesse who asked, "Hey! What do you got in the bag?"

Cleevis told his friend that he had some fish that he'd caught.

"Well," said Jesse, "I'll make you a bet. If I can guess how many fish you have in the bag, you have to give me one. If I can't guess, I'll give you five dollars."

"Sure," said Cleevis enthusiastically. "But you know what? If you can tell me how many fish I have in this bag, I'll give you *both* of them."

"Paw," said Junior, "I'm late for football practice. Could you do my homework for me?"

"Sorry, son," replied his father. "It just wouldn't be right."

"That's okay," replied Junior. "At least you could try."

Drucker

"The only challenge I might accept at this point is to go drifting for catfish."

Jethro had been slipping in and out of a coma for
several months, yet Ellie May stayed by his bedside
every single day. When he came to, he motioned for
her to come closer. As she sat by him, he said, "You
know, Ellie May, you've been with me all through
the bad times. When I got fired from the mill, you
were there. When I lost the farm, you were there to
support me. When I got shot, you were by my side.
When we lost the house, you gave me support.
When my health started failing, you were still by my
side. You know what?"

"What, dear?" Ellie May asked gently.

"I think you bring me bad luck," said Jethro.

Sherman was bragging to J.D. about what a good
dog trainer he was.

"See this hound?" said Sherman. "I taught him to
say the alphabet."

"Really?" said J.D. "That's unbelievable!"

"That's not all," continued his friend. "I taught
him to say it backwards."

"Gee," mused J.D., "even I can't do that. You
must be some teacher."

"Sure am."

"Okay," said J.D. "Let's hear him say it."

"Okay, Rover, say the alphabet backwards."

The dog looked around in silence, ignoring Sherman completely.

"Come on, Rover, say the alphabet," repeated Sherman.

The dog continued to ignore him.

"I thought you said your dog learned the whole alphabet backwards," said J.D.

"I said I taught him," replied Sherman. "I didn't say he learned it."

Q: Why do redneck dogs have flat noses?

A: From chasing parked cars.

A.J. called up Roy Dale to help him move a couch that had become stuck in the doorway. Roy Dale came right over, and the two rednecks pushed and pulled until they were exhausted, but the couch wouldn't budge.

"Forget it," said Roy Dale. "We'll never get this in."

A.J. looked at him quizzically. "In?" he said.

A pickup with two rednecks in it pulled into a lumber yard. A.C. got out and went into the office. "I need some four-by-twos," he said.

"You must mean two-by-fours," said the clerk. A.C. looked blankly at the clerk and scratched his head. "Wait a minute," he said. "I'll go check."

He ran out to the truck, where he had a long conversation with Hank, who was behind the wheel. A.C finally came back in.

"Yeah," he said, "I meant two-by-fours."

"Okay," said the clerk. "How long you want 'em?"

A.C. got the same blank look. "Uh . . . I guess I better go check."

He went back out to the truck, where he had another long conversation with Hank. Finally, A.C. came back into the office.

"A long time," he said. "We're building us a house."

Old Spot had been Cooter's dog for years. Every day when he came in from the fields, Spot met him at the door. This day, however, he came home, and the dog didn't greet him. He looked around and finally found Spot curled up in the corner. He nudged the dog and patted him on the head, but the dog didn't move. Upset, he picked Spot up and carried him to the veterinarian.

"My dog is sick," Cooter told the vet. "Can you help him?"

The vet checked the dog out and said, "I'm sorry to have to tell you, but Spot is dead."

"He can't be," cried Cooter. "Check him again."

The vet checked Spot again, with the same result.

"I'm sorry, Cooter, but your dog is dead."

"Are you absolutely positive?" pleaded Cooter.

"Let me try one more thing," replied the vet. He went into the other room and came back carrying a cat. He put the cat down on the table. The cat jumped up onto the dog's back and began to dig in his nails. Next, the cat jumped on Spot's head and bit his nose. He clawed at the dog's ear, but Spot remained quiet.

"You're right," said Cooter. "My dog is dead. How much do I owe you?"

The vet thought for a second then said, "$545. That's $45 for the office visit, and $500 for the cat scan."

REDNECK HEAVEN

CALDWELL

Q: How did the redneck break his arm raking leaves?

A: He fell out of the tree.

Two old rednecks were playing cards just as they had done every Saturday night for the past fifty years. Jethro had been having trouble remembering which cards were which, and his wife usually had to help him. But not this night. At the end of the game, Bubba said to Jethro, "You did good tonight. You didn't need any help at all with the cards. How come?"

"Well," replied Jethro, "ever since my wife sent me to that memory school, I haven't had any problems at all."

"Memory school?" said Bubba. "What memory school?"

Jethro thought for a moment, "Oh, what do you call that flower that's red and has thorns? It's a real, real pretty flower with a real nice smell?"

"A rose?" asked Bubba.

"Yeah . . . that's it!" Jethro turned to his wife. "Hey, Rose!" he said. "What's the name of that memory school you sent me to?"

"What do you mean by coming home half drunk?" asked Becky Sue as Vern fell through the front door.

"It's not my fault," replied Vern. "I ran out of money."

Willie Fred was showing his friends his new apartment.

"What's that big brass basin for?" asked Peewee, pointing to a sink leaning against a wall.

"That's a talking clock," responded Willie Fred.

"A talking clock?" said Peewee. "I don't believe you. How does it work?"

"Watch," said Willie Fred. He picked up a large hammer lying nearby and took a powerful swing at the basin, which responded with an ear-shattering ring.

Suddenly, a voice from the other side of the wall screamed, "Knock it off, you idiot. It's two A.M.!"

A high school teacher was giving his science class a true/false test. While strolling up and down the aisles, he noticed young Billy Bob, who was flipping a coin, then writing.

"What are you doing?" asked the teacher.

"Getting the answers to the test," replied Billy Bob.

The teacher shook his head and walked on.

A little while later, when everyone had finished, the teacher noticed Billy Bob again flipping the coin.

"Now what are you doing?" asked the teacher.

"Why, I'm checking my answers," replied Billy Bob.

Q: How do rednecks form a car pool?

A: They meet at work.

Doodle walked into Doc Webster's office with a cucumber up his nose, a carrot in his left ear, and a banana in his right ear.

"What's wrong with me?" he asked the doctor frantically.

"It's nothing serious," replied Doc Webster. "You're just not eating properly."

A redneck couple went to the local fairgrounds. Daisy Jean wanted to go up in the ferris wheel, but Clyde didn't, so his wife went on the ride by herself. The wheel went round and round. Suddenly, Daisy Jean was thrown out and landed in a heap at Clyde's feet.

"Are you hurt?" he asked her with concern in his voice.

"Of course I'm hurt!" she replied. "Three times around and you didn't wave even once!"

During World War II, an Englishman, a Frenchman, and a redneck were captured by the Germans and thrown into prison. As luck would have it, the guard was kind and said, "You're going to be locked away for five years, but I'll tell you what I'll do. I'll let you have anything you want now before I lock you away."

The Englishman said, "Give me a five-year supply of beer!" His wish was granted, and he was locked away with his beer.

The Frenchman said, "Give me a five-year supply of brandy!" His wish was also granted, and he was locked away with his brandy.

The redneck said, "Give me a five-year supply of cigarettes!" His wish was granted, too, and he was locked away with his cigarettes.

Five years later, the guard came around to release the prisoners. First, he released the Englishman, who staggered out totally drunk.

Next, the Frenchman was released. He, too, rolled out in a stupor.

Finally, the redneck was released. He walked out, stretched, and said to the guard, "Anybody got a light?"

"I've got a really big sheep farm," bragged Vern.

"Oh, yeah?" said Cleevis. "How many sheep you got?"

"Don't really know," replied Vern. "Every time I try to count them, I fall asleep."

Young Bubba and his classmates had just finished a tour of the local fire station. Before they left, the fire chief quizzed them.

"What happens if your clothes catch on fire?" he asked.

"That's easy," said Bubba. "I don't put them on."

Jimmy Earl was driving his pickup truck past a large country estate when he saw a sign on the gate that read "PLEASE RING BELL FOR THE CARE-TAKER." Jimmy Earl stopped his truck, got out, and rang the bell. When an old man appeared, he asked him, "Are you the caretaker?"

"Yes, I am," replied the old man. "What do you want?"

"Well," said Jimmy Earl, "I'd just like to know why you can't ring the bell for yourself."

Jethro told his parents he was going out to see a movie that he had wanted to see for months, so they were surprised when he returned home in only fifteen minutes.

"What happened?" asked his Maw. "I thought you really wanted to see that movie."

"I did," replied Jethro sadly, "but when I got there, I saw a sign that said 'UNDER 18 NOT ADMITTED,' and I couldn't find seventeen other people to go see it with me."

Mary Beth and J.D. interrupted their vacation to go to the dentist.

"I want a tooth pulled," announced Mary Beth, "and I don't want Novocain because I'm in a big hurry. Just pull the tooth as quickly as possible, and we'll be on our way."

The dentist was impressed. "You're certainly a courageous woman," he said. "Which tooth is it?"

"Show him your tooth, dear," said Mary Beth, turning to J.D.

Billy Joe and Billy Bob were out hunting one sunny day when they happened upon a pretty young girl sunbathing in the nude.

"Boy," said Billy Joe, "she looks good enough to eat."

So Billy Bob shot her.

Q: How do you get a redneck girl to marry you?

A: Tell her she's pregnant.

Freddie Lou was downing a few beers at a local bar
when he looked over and noticed a drunk passed
out at a nearby table. The bartender told him the
drunk was Mr. Miller and asked Freddie Lou if he
could drive Mr. Miller home. Being a good-hearted
sort, Freddie Lou agreed. The bartender wrote down
Mr. Miller's address and gave it to Freddie Lou. The
redneck walked over and tried to wake Mr. Miller,
but the man was groggy and very drunk. Bubba
helped him to his feet, but Mr. Miller fell to the
floor in a heap.

"Brother," thought Freddie Lou. "How could
anyone drink so much?" He took Mr. Miller's arm
and practically dragged him out to the car. He
propped him up against the side of the car while he
looked for his keys, but Mr. Miller quickly slid to the
ground. Freddie Lou found his keys and somehow
managed to get Mr. Miller into the car. He
proceeded to drive to the address the bartender had
given him.

When they arrived, he opened the door on the
passenger side and helped Mr. Miller out. Again,
the drunk fell right to the ground. Cursing to
himself, Freddie Lou helped him to his feet and
practically dragged him to the front door. Mr. Miller
once more fell to the ground as Freddie Lou reached
out to knock on the door. Once again, he helped

him to his feet. Just then, Mrs. Murphy answered the door.

"Hi, Mrs. Murphy," said Freddie Lou. "Your husband had a little too much to drink tonight, so I gave him a ride home."

"Oh, that was so nice of you," said Mrs. Miller, looking around. "But where is his wheelchair?"

Sherman was driving down the road in his pickup truck one day when he happened to look out the window and saw another redneck sitting in a rowboat in a corn field, rowing away for all he's worth. Furious, Sherman got out of the car to tell him off.

"It's rednecks like you that give all of us a bad name," he yelled. "If I knew how to swim, I'd go out there and slap you silly."

J.T. and A.J. were walking in the woods one day.

"Oh, look," said J.T. "Deer tracks!"

"Naw," said A.J., "those are wolf tracks!"

Back and forth they went at each other, arguing over it. Ten minutes later, they were both hit by a train.

Bobby Lee went over to Betty Sue's house for the first time. She showed him into the living room then excused herself to go to the kitchen to make drinks. Looking around the room, he noticed a small vase on the mantel. He picked it up, and just then, Betty Sue walked back in.

"What's this?" asked Bobby Lee.

"Oh, my father's ashes are in there," she replied.

"Oh, gee, I'm sorry," said Bobby Lee. "I didn't mean to show any disrespect."

"It's okay," replied the girl, "he's just too lazy to go to the kitchen to get an ashtray."

Duke went to a carpenter with a special request. "Can you build me a box that is two inches high, two inches wide, and fifty feet long?" he asked.

The carpenter considered the question. "I suppose it could be done," he responded, "but what would you want a box like that for?"

"Well," said Duke, "my neighbor moved away and forgot his garden hose, so he asked me to send it to him."

"Once it catches on, the small-horse household-pet idea will go like blazes. And you may quote Mr. Pudney on that."

YOU KNOW YOU'RE A REDNECK IF...

. . . you've ever taken a beer on a job interview.

. . . your truck has curtains, but your house doesn't.

. . . you wet your bed and ten people immediately know about it.

. . . you have to climb a water tower with a bucket of paint to defend your sister's honor.

. . . you've ever used a weed eater in the house.

. . . your life's ambition is to own a fireworks stand.

A.C. saw a priest walking down the street and noticed his unusual collar. He stopped him and said, "Excuse me, but why are you wearing your shirt backwards?"

The priest laughed, "Because, my son, I am a Father!"

A.C. scratched his head. "I'm a father, too," he said, "and I don't wear my shirt backwards!"

Again the priest laughed. "But I am a Father of thousands!" he explained.

"Well, then," said A.C., "maybe you should wear your shorts backwards instead."

Vern and Buford were walking along opposite sides of a river when they noticed each other.

"Come on over here," said Vern.

"I can't," replied Buford. "I don't know how to swim. Why don't you come over here?"

"I can't swim, either," answered Vern. "What are we gonna do?"

"Wait a second!" said Buford. "I've got an idea. I got a flashlight with me. I'll turn it on, and you walk across the beam to this side."

"No way!" said Vern. "You must think I'm stupid or something. I'll get halfway across, and you'll turn the light off on me!"

Willie Joe was hired by the county to paint the lines down the middle of the road. His first day on the job, he painted ten miles, and his boss was amazed. On the second day, however, he painted just five. The third day, he painted just a single mile of the road. Disappointed in the dropoff in his work, his boss asked what the problem was.

"Well, sir," explained Willie Joe, "every day I have to walk farther and farther to get back to the paint bucket."

Q: Why don't rednecks eat Jell-O?

A: They can't figure out how to get two cups of water into those little packages.

The speeding train came to a sudden, grinding stop.

"What's the matter, conductor?" asked Jethro.

"Nothing much," replied the conductor. "We just ran over a cow."

"Was it on the track?" asked the redneck.

"Nope," replied the annoyed conductor. "We chased it into the barn."

The worst rain in years hit Alabama, and many counties were completely flooded. With the water some six feet deep, one redneck family found itself sitting on the porch roof, watching the wreckage float by. Sammy Dale happened to notice a nice straw hat as it drifted by downstream.

"I'll bet the person who lost that hat is sorry now!" he mused. After the hat floated out of sight around the corner of the house, Sammy Dale continued watching the river. Suddenly, much to his amazement, he spied the hat again, this time floating upstream, against the current! He continued to watch as it floated upstream and around the other corner of the house. After a couple of minutes, it reappeared and started floating back down again. After a while, it came back upstream yet again, rounding the corner of the house. Finally, he couldn't stand it any longer and pointed out the hat to his mother.

"What could be causing that?" asked Sammy Dale.

"Oh, that's Grandpaw," replied his mother. "He said he was going to mow the lawn today, come hell or high water."

Reverend Hill had really gotten into his Sunday sermon. "Stand up if you want to go to heaven!" the preacher exhorted his congregation.

Everyone in the church rose as one, with the exception of Buddy, who was sitting in the front pew.

"Are you telling me you don't want to go to heaven when you die?" thundered the preacher, staring at the redneck.

"When I die, sure," responded Buddy. "I thought you were getting up a load to go right now."

The refrigerator salesman was trying to close a deal by explaining the payment plan.

"You make a small down payment," he explained, "and then you don't make any more payments for six months."

Buford looked amazed. "Who told you about us?" he asked.

Hank and Joe Bob were walking down a country road when Hank exclaimed, "Aw, look, there's a dead bird."

"Where?" said Joe Bob, looking up.

"No, I can't tell you how to get to 'Lost Lake'!
Nobody can. That's why they call it Lost Lake!"

Little Bobby liked to hang out at the old country store much of the day. The owner, Mr. Jones, noticed how the other boys would tease him and make fun of him. They'd say he was dumber than dirt, and to prove it, they'd offer Bobby his choice between a nickel and a dime. He always took the nickel, they said, because it was bigger. One day, after Bobby again grabbed the nickel, Mr. Jones took him off to one side and said, " Bobby, those boys are making fun of you. They think you don't know that a dime is worth more than a nickel. How come you take the nickel each time? Is it because it's bigger?"

"Nope," explained Bobby. "It's just that if I took the dime, they'd quit doing it!"

Two redneck bowling teams chartered a double-decker bus to take them to a tournament in Atlantic City. One team was in the bottom level of the bus, while the other team was in the top level. The team down below was singing and laughing when Bubba realized he didn't hear anything from the top. He walked up the stairs and found all the guys from the second team clutching the seats in front of them with white knuckles, scared to death.

"What the heck's goin' on?" he said. "We're down there havin' a grand old time."

"Sure," called out Jethro from the back row. "You guys got a driver."

Young Junior was late for Sunday school. Since he was usually very prompt, his teacher asked him if anything was wrong.

"Well, I was going to go fishing," replied the boy, "but my paw told me that I needed to go to church."

The teacher was very impressed and asked him if his dad had explained why it was more important to go to church than to go fishing.

"Yup," replied Junior. "Paw said he didn't have enough bait for both of us."

Q: Why do rednecks have TGIF printed on their shoes?

A: Toes Go In First.

The redneck reserve unit was being inspected by the captain. When the review was finished, the captain told the sergeant that everything was fine except for one thing.

"Your soldiers smell horrible," he said. "You should have them change their underwear."

"Yes, sir," replied the sergeant as the captain walked away. Turning to his troops, he told them what the captain had said.

"Okay, now," he went on, "Jimmy Ray, you change with J.T. Billy Joe, you change with Elroy . . . "

A rather inebriated Bo was staggering home with a pint of booze in his back pocket when he slipped and fell down heavily. He managed to get to his feet but felt something wet running down his leg.

"Please, God," he begged, "let it be blood!"

Fern went for her first job interview in an office. The interviewer decided to start off with the basics.

"So, Miss," he said, "can you tell us your age, please?"

Fern counted carefully on her fingers before she answered. "Twenty-two," she said.

The interviewer tried another easy one to break the ice.

"Can you tell us your height, please?"

Fern stood up and took out a measuring tape from her handbag. She held one end with her foot and extended the tape to the top of her head. She checked the measurement then announced, "Five feet, two inches."

The interviewer began to think she might not be the person for the job, but just to be sure, he asked her the most basic question.

"Just to confirm our records, what is your name, please?"

Fern bobbed her head from side to side for about twenty seconds, mouthing something silently to herself before replying, "Fern!"

"Just out of curiosity, Miss," the interviewer said, "I can understand your counting on your fingers to work out your age, and the measuring tape for your height is obvious enough, but what were you doing when I asked you your name?"

"Oh, that," replied Fern, "I was just running through, 'Happy birthday to you, happy birthday to you . . .' "

A big-city lawyer was representing the railroad in a lawsuit filed by an old rancher. The rancher's prize bull was missing from the section of his ranch where the railroad passed through. The rancher wanted to be paid the fair value of the bull. Before the case began, the attorney for the railroad cornered the rancher and tried to get him to settle out of court. The lawyer did his best selling job, and finally the rancher agreed to take half of what he was asking. After the rancher had signed the release form and taken the check, the young lawyer couldn't help but gloat a little over his success.

"You know," he said to the rancher, "I hate to tell you this, but I really put one over on you. There's no way I could've have won the case. The train's engineer was asleep at the switch and the fireman was back in the caboose when the train went through your ranch that day. I didn't have a single witness to put on the stand. I bluffed you!"

"Well," replied the old rancher, "to tell you the truth, young feller, I was a little worried about winning that case myself. That darned bull came home this morning."

Jesse and his paw, two rednecks from the backwoods country, were visiting their first modern mall. They were amazed by everything they saw, but especially by two shiny, silver walls that moved apart and came back together again.

"What in the world is that, Paw?" asked Jesse.

"Jesse," responded his father, "I ain't never seen nothing like that in all my life. I don't know what it is!"

While Jesse and Paw watched, wide-eyed, an old lady in a wheelchair rolled up to the moving silver walls and pressed a button. The walls opened up, and the lady rolled between them into a small room. The walls closed behind her, and Jesse and Paw watched as small circles of lights with numbers in them lit up above the walls. They continued to watch as the circles lit up in the reverse direction. Soon, the walls opened up again and a gorgeous young woman stepped out.

"I sure don't know what that is," said Paw to Jesse, "but go get your maw."

Q: Why do rednecks use so much shampoo?

A: The instructions read: LATHER, RINSE, REPEAT.

J.D. and Elroy decided one day that they wanted to learn how to ice fish. They went to the local tackle shop and spent a thousand dollars on the latest ice-fishing equipment. Off they went to Lake Winnebago, where they cut a hole in the ice and spent several hours setting up their gear and catching nothing. Some more time passed. Then an old-timer walked past them with just a bamboo rod. He proceeded to drill a hole in the ice about ten feet from them and immediately began to catch fish. J.D. went over and asked the old man what his secret was, but he just glared at him and mumbled something unintelligible. Thinking the old man might be upset because they were at his favorite spot, J.D. walked away.

The old man continued to catch fish, and finally Elroy decided to ask him for his secret. He went to the old-timer and said, "Hey, I'm sorry if we took your spot, but could you tell us your secret? We're new and have never done this."

The old man again glared and said, "Hmm-mmmphhhhrrrrppphhhermmmmm."

"What was that again?" asked Elroy.

The old man spit something into his hand and yelled, "I said you gotta keep your worms warm!"

"Don't I know you from somewhere?"

A farmer and his brand-new bride were riding home from the chapel in a wagon pulled by a team of horses when the older horse stumbled. The farmer glared at him and said, "That's one."

A little further along, the poor old horse stumbled again. The farmer glared and said, "That's two."

A few minutes later, the poor old horse stumbled again. The farmer said, "That's three," reached under his seat, pulled out a shotgun, and shot the horse.

His bride took all this in in horror.

"How could you do that?" she asked. "That was a simply awful thing to do."

"That's one," said the farmer with a glare.

Roy Dale, Bobby Joe, and Vern decided to take a trip to California for their vacation. They were driving through the desert when their car suddenly ran out of gas. They all decided to start walking to the nearest town, some fifty miles back, to get help.

A rancher was sitting on his front porch that evening when he saw Roy Dale top the horizon and walk toward him. The rancher noticed the redneck was carrying a glass of water, so when he got within hearing distance, he called out, "Hey, there. Why are you carrying a glass of water through the desert?"

Roy Dale told him his dilemma and explained that since he had a long way to go, he might get thirsty, so that's why he was carrying the water.

A little while later, the rancher noticed Bobby Joe walking toward him with a sandwich in his hand.

"What are you doing with that sandwich?" asked the rancher.

Bobby Joe told him his predicament and said that since he had a long way to go, he might get hungry, and that's why he had the sandwich.

Finally Vern appeared on the horizon, dragging a car door through the sand. The rancher couldn't contain his curiosity.

"Hey, why are you dragging that car door?" he asked.

"Well," replied Vern, "I have a long way to go, so if it gets too hot, I'll roll down the window."

Q: Why did the redneck get fired from the M&M factory?

A: He threw out all the Ws.

Doodle, Billy Ray, and Elroy were prisoners of war scheduled to be executed by a German firing squad during World War II. The Germans brought out Doodle and stood him in front of a pole. Suddenly, he pointed behind them and shouted, "Tornado!" They all turned around to see, and Doodle ran away.

Next, they put Billy Ray in front of the firing squad. Just as they got ready to shoot, he yelled, "Earthquake!" The Germans all hit the ground, and Billy Ray escaped.

Finally, it was Elroy's turn. Just as the firing squad got ready to shoot, he looked around and shouted, "Fire!"

Being a good grandson, Clyde decided to visit his elderly grandmother. While he was talking to her, he began nibbling on some peanuts in a bowl on the coffee table. After a few minutes, he had finished them all off. When it was time to leave, he turned to his grandmother and said, "It was good to see you again, Gram. And thanks for the peanuts."

"That's okay," the old woman replied. "Since I lost my dentures, I can only suck the chocolate off 'em anyway."

Q: If a redneck and a northerner jump off a building at the same time, who will hit the ground first?

A: The northerner. The redneck will stop to ask for directions.

Three mental patients were being considered for release from an institution. The head doctor came to ask them all a question to judge if they were ready to rejoin the outside world. The first patient entered the room.

"How much is two plus two?" asked the doctor.

"Five thousand!" answered the patient.

"I'm sorry," replied the doctor. "That's not correct."

The second patient entered. Again the doctor asked, "How much is two plus two?"

"Tuesday!" answered the second patient.

"I'm sorry," replied the doctor. "That's not correct."

Jethro, the third patient, entered the room. Again the doctor asked, "How much is two plus two?"

"Four," answered Jethro. The doctor is delighted and asked how he got the answer.

"That's easy," responded "I just divided five thousand by Tuesday!"

Two years later, Louie—the second patient—got another chance. He was told he'd be able to leave, but first he had to pass a test. The doctor called him in and asked him to name the parts of his body.

"Finger, hand, wrist, knee . . . ," said Louie, but he pointed to his elbow when he said knee, and his stomach when he said finger. He failed the test and had to wait two more years before he got another chance. This time he said, "Shoulder, arm, toe, ear . . . ," but pointed to his nose when he said toe. He failed again. He also failed on his next four tries. Finally, after nearly twenty years in the institution, he came in and said, "Finger, hand, wrist, elbow, shoulder, eye, nose, mouth." He got every one right, so they told him he could leave. Before he went, however, they asked him how he finally got it right.

"Easy," said Louie, pointing to his head. "I just used my kidneys."

Luke and Scooter stopped at a gas station to fill up their pickup truck. On the side of the building, they saw a sign saying "ENTER HERE FOR A CHANCE AT FREE SEX!" They hurried inside and asked the attendant how to enter.

"All you gotta do," said the attendant, "is guess a number between one and ten."

"Okay," said Luke. "Five."

"Sorry," said the attendant. "The number was eight."

Scooter stepped up next to try his luck.

"Seven," he guessed.

"Sorry," said the attendant. "The number was three."

The two rednecks got back in their truck and drove away. As they sped down the road, Scooter turned to Luke and said, "You know, I think that contest was rigged."

"Nope, it's on the up and up," said Luke. "Last week, my wife won twice."

Young Junior and Johnny Lee were camping out in the forest. The mosquitoes were so fierce that the boys had to hide under their blankets to keep from being bitten. All of a sudden, Junior saw some lightning bugs.

"We might as well give up," he said to Johnny Lee. "Now they're coming at us with flashlights!"

Ida Mae, Peggy Sue, and Becky Lou went to a bar to have a drink.

"I'll have a B and C," said Ida Mae to the bartender.

"What's a B and C?" he asked.

"Bourbon and Coke," replied Ida Mae.

"I'll have a G and T," said Peggy Sue.

"What's a G and T?" asked the bartender.

"Gin and tonic," she replied.

"And I'll have a 15," said Becky Lou.

"What's a 15?" he asked.

"7 and 7," replied Becky Lou.

Davy Roy came home from work early one day and found his wife in bed with a total stranger.

"What on earth do you think you're doing?" he screamed.

The wife turned to the other man. "See," she said. "I told you he was stupid."

Furious, Davy Roy rushed to the cupboard, pulled out his gun, and put it to his head. "I'm going to kill myself!" he told her. His wife just started laughing.

"Don't laugh!" he screamed. "You're next!"

"Uncle Whit was country when country wasn't cool."

Aunt Emma and Uncle Jeb went to the doctor for a checkup. Uncle Jeb went in first. When the doctor finished with him, he sent the old man back into the waiting room and called Aunt Emma in.

"Before I examine you," he said, "I'd like to talk about your husband first."

"Oh, no," said Aunt Emma. "I knew it. It's his heart. I told him to lay off the eggs."

"No, no," the doctor said. "He's all right physically, but I'm worried about his mental health."

"Whatever do you mean?" asked Aunt Emma.

"Well," explained the doctor, "I asked him how he's feeling and he told me he felt great. He said that when he got up to go the bathroom at night, he opened the door and God turned the light on for him. When he was finished, he'd shut the door and God would turn the light back off for him."

"Oh, that's no big deal" said Aunt Emma, relieved. "He's just peeing in the fridge again!"

A redneck scientist was conducting an important experiment in animal behavior. He first trained a frog to leap forward when he gave the command "Jump." Next, he removed one of the frog's front legs and repeated the command. The frog jumped again. He then removed the frog's other front leg. When he repeated the command, the frog jumped once more. He repeated the experiment after removing one of the frog's back legs with the same result. Finally, he removed the frog's last leg. When he commanded it to jump, nothing happened. He summarized his findings in his journal as follows:

"When one of a frog's legs is cut off, the frog is still able to jump.

"When two of a frog's legs are cut off, the frog is still able to jump.

"When three of a frog's legs are cut off, the frog is still able to jump.

"When all four of a frog's legs are cut off, however, the frog suddenly goes deaf."

Q: What do you call a redneck with a third grade education?

A: Professor.

The new mailman was greeted by a boy and a huge dog.

"Does your dog bite?" asked the mailman.

"Nope," replied the boy.

The mailman proceeded to take two steps forward, and the dog suddenly snapped at him, nipping him on the leg.

"Hey," yelled the mailman. "I thought you said your dog doesn't bite!"

"He doesn't," replied the boy. "That's not my dog!"

Buford was fishing through a hole in the ice. After half an hour had passed, he had nothing to show for his efforts. He decided that maybe the fish were staying in some other area, so he drilled another hole. After another wasted half hour, he again moved and started drilling yet another hole. Suddenly, he heard a deep voice from somewhere above him say, "THERE ARE NO FISH UNDER THE ICE!" Buford paused for a moment, then continued drilling the hole. Again came the voice: "THERE ARE NO FISH UNDER THE ICE!"

In awe, Buford stopped and said, "Is that you, God?"

"NO," answered the voice. "THIS IS THE MANAGER OF THE ICE RINK. THERE ARE NO FISH UNDER THE ICE!"

Young Joe's chemistry teacher wanted to teach his ninth grade class a lesson about the evils of liquor. He produced a glass of water, a glass of whiskey, and two worms.

"Now, class," he began, "observe closely." He proceeded to put one of the worms into the glass of water. The worm in the water swam about, happy as could be.

The second worm he put into the glass filled with whiskey. The worm swam about for a moment, then started shaking before quickly sinking to the bottom, as dead as dead could be.

"Now," he asked, "what lesson can we learn from this experiment?"

"That's easy," replied Joe. "Drink whiskey and you won't get worms."

The night that Jesse and Nadine got married, the young bride put a foot locker in their bedroom. She locked it and put the key on a chain that hung around her neck. For the next fifty years, Jesse tried to figure out what was in the locker, but Nadine always changed the subject, never giving him a straight answer. Finally, on the night of their fiftieth wedding anniversary, Jesse said to her, " Nadine, I've got to know what's in that trunk!"

"Oh, all right," said Nadine. She took the key and unlocked the foot locker. There inside were two ears of corn and $25,000.

"I don't understand," said Jesse. "What's with the two ears of corn?"

"Well," said Nadine, "in the fifty years that we've been married, every time I broke our marriage vows, I put an ear of corn in the trunk."

Jesse was upset at first, then thought to himself, "Twice in fifty years . . . I guess that's not so bad."

Then he said, "And what about the $25,000?"

"Well," said Nadine, "every time I got a bushel, I sold it."

Q: What do you call a redneck's cow that's just had a baby?

A: Decalfinated.

YOU KNOW YOU'RE A REDNECK IF...

. . . when you see a sign that reads "Say No to Crack," it reminds you to pull your pants up.

. . . your Christmas tree has beef jerky ornaments.

. . . your senior prom has a day care center.

. . . your two-year-old has more teeth than you do.

. . . your wedding song is "Ninety-nine Bottles of Beer on the Wall."

. . . you think a beer belly is sexy.

. . . you've ever eaten roadkill.

. . . when someone asks how you are, you respond, "fair to middlin."

Jackson was in extremely rough shape. He constantly gasped for breath, and his eyes bulged. His doctors didn't know what was wrong with him, but after exhaustive tests, they decided he didn't have very long to live. Jackson decided to live it up and make the most of the time he had left. He withdrew all his money from the bank and went on one final shopping spree. His last stop of the day was at the most expensive haberdashery in the city. Jackson told the clerk he wanted a dozen of the finest silk shirts.

"I wear a size fourteen," he told the salesman.

"Your neck looks bigger than fourteen," replied the clerk. "I'd say you need a size sixteen."

"I know my size," insisted Jackson. "I've been wearing a size fourteen for twenty years, and I want them in a fourteen."

"Okay," replied the clerk. "I'll get them for you, but I've got to warn you, if you wear a size fourteen, you'll gasp all day long and your eyes will bulge out."

Why did the redneck put his finger over the nail when he was hammering?

A: The noise was giving him a headache.

"*Now don't expect miracles, you're white trash.*"

It was a beautiful summer morning when Tommy burst into the living room and said, "Maw! Paw! I have some great news for you! I'm getting married to the most beautiful girl in town. She only lives a block away, and her name is Becky."

After dinner that night, Tommy 's father took him aside.

"Son," he began, "I have something to tell you. Your mother and I have been married for thirty years. She's a wonderful wife and mother. She was never very exciting in the bedroom, however, so I used to fool around a lot with other women. Becky is actually your half-sister, so I'm afraid you can't marry her."

Tommy was heartbroken, but he eventually started dating again. A year later he came home and proudly announced to his parents, "I have great news! Emmy said yes! We're going to get married next June." Again, Tommy's father insisted on a private conversation with his son and broke the bad news.

"I'm afraid Emmy is your half-sister, too, Tommy. I'm really sorry about this."

Tommy was furious! He decided to tell his mother the news his father had shared with him.

"I guess I'm never going to get married," he complained. "Every time I fall in love, Dad tells me the girl is my half-sister."

His mother smiled and shook her head. "Don't pay any attention to what he says," she advised. "He's not really your father."

A fellow from the city drove his car into a ditch on a desolated stretch of road down south. Luckily for him, a local farmer happened by with his big strong horse named Buddy.

"Don't you worry none," said the farmer. "Buddy and me will get your car out of that ditch."

He hitched Buddy up to the car and yelled, "Pull, Nellie, pull!" Buddy didn't move an inch. Then the farmer hollered, "Pull, Buster, pull!" Again, the horse didn't respond. Once more the farmer commanded, "Pull, Bossy, pull!" Nothing. Finally, the farmer said, "Pull, Buddy, pull!" The horse dragged the car out of the ditch with no problem whatsoever. The motorist was most appreciative, but at the same time, very curious.

"Can I ask you something? Why did you call your horse by the wrong name three times?" he asked.

"Oh," replied the farmer, "Old Buddy here is blind. If he thought he was the only one pulling, he wouldn't even try."

Bo and Cliff decided to try their hand at fishing. Having never done so before, they decided to go all the way. They spent a small fortune buying all the equipment they needed, including fancy new reels, rods, and tackle boxes. Next, they rented a beautiful cabin in the woods for a week, paying top dollar. Finally, they bought some bait, rented a boat, and paddled out to catch their supper.

On the first day, they didn't catch a thing. The same thing happened on the second day and the third. It went on like this all week until finally, on the last day of their vacation, Cliff managed to catch a fish. That night, driving home with their catch, they were really depressed. Cliff turned to Bo and said, "Do you realize that this one lousy fish we caught cost us more than fifteen hundred dollars?"

"Wow!" exclaimed Bo. "It's a good thing we didn't catch any more."

Luke had recently gotten his pilot's license, and he decided to take A.J. out with him for a spin. They were coming in for a landing at a neighboring airport, and A.J. noticed that Luke was a nervous wreck. His face was bright red, and he was sweating profusely. He brought the plane down and instantly came to a screeching halt. Luke turned to A.J. and said, "Wow! That was the shortest runway I ever did land on."

"Yeah," replied A.J., "and so wide."

Jethro and Bubba were fishing in an inlet in their motorboat, when they saw another boat coming in loaded with fish. Since they hadn't had any luck themselves, Jethro asked the fisherman what his secret was.

"Just go all the way out to sea until the water gets fresh," he replied. "Stop there and drop yer line."

Sure that their luck was about to change, Jethro fired up the motor and headed out to sea. When they got a mile out, he told Bubba to fill up a bucket and taste the water.

"It's still salty," said Bubba. Jethro went out another couple of miles and told Bubba to taste the water again.

"It's still salty," came the response. They went on like this for several hours. Finally, as it was starting to get dark and they were in the middle of nowhere, Jethro told Bubba to taste the water one final time.

"Can't, Jethro," said Bubba. "There ain't no more water in the bucket."

DID YOU HEAR ABOUT...

. . . the redneck who injured himself tap dancing?
He broke his ankle when he fell into the sink.

. . . the redneck who was polishing the flagpole? He
varnished into thin air!

. . . the redneck who stayed up all night to see
where the sun went? It finally dawned on him.

. . . the redneck who was so dumb, he thought the
International Dateline was a 1-900 number?

. . . the redneck who was in a spelling bee? He was
asked to spell Mississippi and said, "Which one?
The river or the state?"

. . . the redneck who drained his pool? His wife
asked him why he did it, and he told her, "I
want to practice diving but I don't know how
to swim."

Billy Bob and a farmer named Roy were on death row in an Alabama prison. When their last appeals were turned down, the warden came in with the bad news.

"Well, boys," he said, "it's your time to die. You're each allowed one last request."

The two men thought for a minute, then Billy Bob said, "Warden, for my last request, I'd like to hear 'Achey-Breaky Heart' just one more time."

Not being a country-and-western fan, the warden cringed, then nodded.

"Okay," he said. He turned to the farmer and asked, "And what's your last request?"

Roy shuddered and said, "Warden, can I go first?"

While out for a ride in their car, Aunt Vera and Uncle Lem stopped at a roadside restaurant for lunch. Aunt Vera left her glasses on the table, but didn't realize it until they had driven for a half hour more on the highway. They found a place to turn around and headed back. Uncle Lem fussed and complained all the way back to the restaurant. When they finally arrived, Aunt Vera got out of the car to get her glasses.

"As long as you're going in there," said Uncle Lem, "you might as well get my hat, too."

Brothers Jackson and Cleevis, ages eight and ten, respectively, were always getting into trouble. Anytime anything went wrong in the neighborhood, you could be sure Jackson and Cleevis had a hand in it. Their parents didn't know what to do to control them. Nothing they tried had any effect. Hearing about Father Murphy, who worked with delinquent boys, the mother suggested to her husband that they ask the priest to talk to the boys. The brothers' father agreed. The mother went to Father Murphy and asked for his help.

"Of course," he said. "Let me see young Jackson first."

The mother sent Jackson in to see the priest. Father Murphy had the boy sit across from him. He himself sat behind a large, impressive desk. Father Murphy and Jackson sat and stared at each other for five minutes without saying anything. Finally, the priest pointed his finger at the boy and asked in a deep voice, "Where is God?"

Jackson looked under the desk, in the corners of the room, and all around him, but said nothing. Again, the priest pointed at the boy and repeated even louder, "Where is God?"

Just as before, Jackson looked all around but said nothing. Finally, a third time, Father Murphy leaned across the desk, put his forefinger almost onto the boy's nose, and thundered, "Where is God?"

The boy panicked, ran out of the room, and sped home. He found Cleevis and dragged him upstairs where they could be alone.

"We are in big trouble," he said in a trembling voice.

"What do you mean, big trouble?" asked Cleevis.

"God is missing," answered Jackson, "and they think we did it!"

Ike and Clyde went out bear hunting. Ike stayed in the cabin while Clyde went out searching for a bear. He soon found a huge grizzly and shot at it, but only managed to wound it. The enraged bear charged Clyde, who dropped his rifle and started running as fast as he could for the cabin. The bear was just a little bit faster, and the distance between the two closed. Just as Clyde reached the open cabin door, he tripped and fell flat on his face. The bear, being too close behind to stop, tripped over him and went rolling into the cabin. Clyde jumped up, closed the cabin door, and yelled to Ike, inside, "You skin this one while I go get another!"

Abner and Jed ran into each other for the first time in twenty years, and began to catch up on their lives.

"I heard you just got married again," said Abner.

"Yup," said Jed. "For the fourth time."

"The fourth time?" responded Abner. "What happened to your first three wives?"

"They all died, Ab."

"That's a shame," said Abner. "How did they die?"

"Well," said Jed, "my first wife ate poison mushrooms."

"That's terrible!" replied his friend. "And your second?"

"Same thing," he said. "She ate poison mushrooms."

"Did your third eat poison mushrooms, too?" asked Abner.

"Oh, no," answered Jed. "She died of a broken neck."

"I see," said Abner. "An accident."

"Nope," said Jed. "Wouldn't eat her mushrooms."

Q: Why don't rednecks call 911 in an emergency?

A: They can't find "eleven" on the phone dial.

Buck spent the evening tossing down a number of beers at the local bar. It was after eleven o'clock when he finally staggered out into the cold and rainy night in an attempt to find his way home. With the weather as bad as it was, he soon became lost, and found himself wandering through the town cemetery. He slipped while walking and fell headlong into a freshly dug grave. In his condition, the rain and mud proved too much to handle, and he couldn't manage to climb out. "Help!" he cried out. "Help! I'm so cold!"

A little while later, another well-oiled patron left the bar. As luck would have it, the second man was nearby when he heard Buck cry.

"Help, I'm so cold!" Buck continued to call. The other man staggered in the direction of the voice. It got louder and louder as he neared the cemetery.

"Help! I'm cold! Help! I'm cold!"

The second man followed the voice and approached the grave. As he peered over the side, Buck looked up and yelled one more time, "Help! I'm cold!"

"Of course you're cold," replied the second drunk, peering down. "You've kicked off all your dirt."

One day, young Webster asked his mother how old she was. She told him that little boys didn't ask ladies how old they were. He then asked her how much she weighed. She told him that little boys didn't ask ladies how much they weighed. Not to be denied in his quest for knowledge, he finally asked her why she and his daddy had gotten a divorce. His mother told him that little boys didn't ask ladies personal questions like that.

Later that day, Webster was playing with young Cooter. He told him that his mother wouldn't tell him how old she was or how much she weighed or anything. Cooter told him that all he had to do was look on his mother's driver's license and he could find out anything he wanted to know. Webster rushed home, got his mother's purse, and looked at her driver's license. He then went and told his mother he knew all about her.

"I know you're thirty years old," he said. "And I know you weigh 125 pounds." Saving the best for last, he finished, "I also know you got divorced from daddy because you got an F in sex!"

THE HAZARDS OF
SELF-TATTOOING

Rush Limbaugh and his chauffeur were out driving in the country when they accidentally hit and killed a pig that had wandered out onto the road. Limbaugh told the chauffeur to drive to the farm and apologize to the farmer.

They approached the farmhouse, and the chauffeur got out and knocked on the front door. He was let in by the farmer and remained inside for what seemed like hours. When he finally came out and went back to the car, Limbaugh asked him why he had been so long.

"Well," replied the chauffeur, "first the farmer shook my hand, then he offered me a beer, then his wife brought me some cookies, and his daughter showered me with kisses."

"That's strange," said Limbaugh. "What did you tell the farmer?"

"I told him that I was Rush Limbaugh's driver," answered the chauffeur, "and that I just killed the pig."

Q: Why don't rednecks eat pickles?

A: Because they can't get their head in the jar.

Thelma Lou, in her late fifties, was walking down the street one day. She was still well-dressed, but she was beginning to show some wear. Suddenly, a halo appeared around the sun, and she heard a heavenly voice whisper in her ear, "Thou shalt live another fifty years."

"Well," she muttered to herself, "If I'm going to be around for another fifty years, I may as well enjoy myself." She decided to get a face lift, a tummy tuck, and a nose job. Six months later, after the last surgical procedure had been completed, she looked like a million bucks. Whistling a happy tune as she left the hospital, she stepped off the curb and was immediately run over by a speeding garbage truck. When she opened her eyes, the Lord stood in front of her.

"God," she cried, "how come You let that truck hit me after promising me another fifty years of life?"

"Sorry, lady," replied the Lord. "I didn't recognize you."

Father Murphy was walking down the street one day when he saw young Remy jumping and trying to reach a doorbell. The priest asked the boy if he needed help.

"Yes," answered Remy. The priest reached up and pushed the bell for him.

"What next?" asked Father Murphy.

"Run like hell!" responded the youngster, running away.

Mattie Lou called in a repairman to fix her television. Just as he finished, she heard her husband, Jed, put his key in the front door lock.

"Hurry," she said to the repairman, "you'll have to hide. My husband is insanely jealous." Since there was no time to run out the back door, the repairman hid inside the TV console. Jed came in and immediately plopped down in his favorite chair to watch some football. Inside the TV, the repairman was squeezed together, getting hotter and hotter by the second. Finally, he couldn't stand it anymore. He climbed out, marched across the room, and went out the front door. Jed looked at the TV set, looked at his wife, looked back at the set again.

"I didn't see the referee send that guy off the field," he said. "Did you?"

Luke, a farmer, who was originally from the city, was out plowing his field one day when his tractor got stuck in the wet ground. An old-timer driving by stopped his truck and walked over to the fence.

"You need a mule to plow such wet ground," he said.

"Do you know where I can buy one?" asked Luke.

"Well," said the old man, "I just happen to have one for a hundred dollars."

"I'll take him," said Luke, counting out the money.

"I can't bring him over today," said the old-timer, pocketing the money. "But I'll have him over to you tomorrow for sure."

The next day, the truck pulled up and the old farmer got out.

"Sorry," he said, "but I got some bad news. I went out after breakfast this morning and I found the mule dead."

"Well," said the city feller, "then just give me my money back."

"Can't do that," said the old-timer apologetically. "I went and spent it already."

"OK," said Luke. "Then just unload the mule."

"What ya gonna do with him?" asked the old man.

"I think I'll raffle him off," replied Luke.

"You can't raffle off a dead mule!" chuckled the farmer.

"Oh, yeah?" said Luke. "Watch me. I just won't tell anybody he's dead."

A month went by, and the city fella and the farmer ran into each other at the barber shop.

"What ever happened with that dead mule?" the old man asked.

"I raffled him off," said Luke. "I sold a hundred tickets at two dollars apiece and made a ninety-eight dollar profit."

"Didn't anyone complain?" asked the old-timer.

"Just the guy who won," said Luke, "so I gave him his two dollars back."

Huck called the police station and explained breathlessly, "There's a man lying in the middle of the road on Sycamore Street who was hit by a pickup truck. He needs an ambulance real bad."

"Just a moment," replied the dispatcher. "How do you spell the name of that street?"

Huck thought for a minute. "Uh, S-I-C-K . . . no, uh, C-Y-C-O . . . no," he struggled. "I'll tell you what. I'll just drag him over to Lee Street and you can pick him up over there."

Tucker didn't like the congressman from a nearby district. One day, he got into his car and drove into the heart of the legislator's hometown. He quickly found a bar and, after a few beers, summoned up the courage to do something he had wanted to do for years. He stood up in the bar and yelled, "Your congressman is a horse's behind."

No sooner had he said it than a large, mean-looking bouncer marched over, picked him up, and tossed him out the door.

Not one to back down from a fight, Tucker returned to the bar, had another beer or two, and repeated his statement even louder. Again, he was unceremoniously tossed out the door.

"Why can't I say your congressman is a horse's behind?" he protested. "This is a free country, isn't it?"

"Sure is, mister," said the bouncer. "But this is also horse country."

Jefferson, Tucker's cousin from the big city, was trying to show Uncle Jim how smart he was.

"I've been told that you old backwoodsmen are pretty smart even though you haven't had much schooling," said Jefferson.

"That's right," said Jim.

"Well, sir, I'm a college student, and I wonder if you would mind having a contest with me to see which of us is smarter?"

"Wouldn't mind at all," replied Jim. "What do you got in mind?"

"How about if we take turns asking each other questions," said Jefferson, "until one of us can't answer?"

"Okay," said Jim, "and what are the stakes?"

"Well," said Jefferson, "if you want to play for money, how about one dollar a question?"

"Seems to me," said Jim, "with you being a college student and all, that you should put up a dollar while I put up fifty cents."

"That's fine with me," replied Jefferson. "You start."

"Okay," said Jim. After thinking for a few moments, he asked, "What has three legs, is purple, and barks like a dog?"

"I don't know," replied Jefferson, after thinking hard for a few seconds. "Here's your dollar. But tell me, what does have three legs, is purple, and barks like a dog?"

"Danged if I know," said Jim. "Here's your fifty cents."

Q: What do you get when you offer a redneck girl a penny for her thoughts?

A: Change.

When Biff's father died, Biff—who lived far away—called his brother Cade and told him, "Do something nice for Paw and send me the bill."

A week later, he got a bill for two hundred dollars, which he paid. The next month, he got another bill for two hundred dollars, which he also paid, assuming it was some related expense. Bills for two hundred dollars kept arriving every month, however, and Biff called his brother to find out what was going on.

"Well," said Cade, "you said to do something nice for Paw."

"Yes," said Biff.

"So I rented him a tuxedo," replied his brother.

While little Ike was at school one day, his pet cat ran out into the street and was killed in traffic. His mother was concerned about how he would take the news. When he arrived home, she explained the tragedy and tried to console the boy, saying, "But don't worry, the cat is in heaven with God now."

"So what?" replied the boy. "What's God gonna do with a dead cat?"

While out walking one day, Ulee found a lamp and decided to rub the dust off. Sure enough, as soon as he rubbed it, a genie appeared. The genie told Ulee he would grant him three wishes.

"But there's one condition," said the genie. "Everything you wish for, your mother-in-law will get double."

Ulee's first wish was for ten million dollars. The genie reminded him that his mother-in-law would get twenty million dollars.

"That's okay with me," replied Ulee.

His next wish was for a house by the sea. Again, the genie reminded him that his mother-in-law would get two houses by the sea. Again, Ulee said, "That's okay."

"It is done," said the genie. "What now is your third wish?"

Ulee thought long and hard. Finally, he announced, "I want to be beaten half to death."

Whenever young Robbie was out with his mother, he would embarrass her whenever nature called by announcing loud and clear, "I have to pee."

"I wish you wouldn't say that," she told him. "From now on, instead of saying 'I have to pee,' say, 'I have to whisper.'"

This worked fine, until one day when Robbie was in school. He felt the urge but was embarrassed to tell his teacher. His teacher could tell something was bothering him and called him up to her desk.

"What's the matter, Robbie?" she asked him. Poor Robbie looked around to see if anyone was looking at him.

"It's all right," she told him. "There's nothing to be ashamed about. Come here. You can whisper in my ear."

Q: What did the redneck name his pet zebra?

A: Spot.

Billy Bob and Bobbie Sue had just gotten married and were spending their honeymoon in his daddy's hunting cabin in the woods. After a romantic meal, he carried her across the threshold, and they got into bed. Just as they started getting amorous, Bobbie Sue whispered in his ear, "Billy Bob, please be gentle. I ain't never been with a man before."

Billy Bob sat up in bed with an amazed look on his face. "What?" he shouted.

"That's right," she repeated. "I've never been with a man before."

Billy Bob jumped out of bed, grabbed his clothes, and raced out the door and into his pickup truck. He drove straight to his parent's house, rushed inside, and started screaming, "Hey, Daddy! Hey, Paw! Get up! Get up!"

His father rushed downstairs and gasped, "Billy Bob, what are you doin' here?"

Breathing hard from his mad rush, Billy Bob gasped, "Well, Bobbie Sue an' I was in the cabin, and she told me she ain't never been with a man before, so I rushed right outta there and came back here as quick as I could!"

"Son, you done the right thing," he said. "If she ain't good enough for her own family, she sure ain't good enough for ours!"

Q. What do they call "Hee Haw" in Arkansas?

A. A documentary.

Emmy Lou jumped up to answer the telephone when it rang. She listened with relief to the kindly voice in her ear.

"How are you, darling?" it said. "What kind of a day are you having?"

"Oh, mother," said Emmy Lou, breaking down into tears, "it's been such a bad day. The baby is sick, and the washing machine broke down. I haven't had a chance to do any shopping because I just sprained my ankle and I'm hobbling around. Even worse, the house is a mess and I'm having company for dinner tonight!"

The mother was shocked and very sympathetic. "Don't cry, now, darling," she said. "Everything will be fine. Just sit down, relax, and close your eyes. I'll be over in a few minutes. I'll do your shopping, clean up the house, and cook dinner for you. I'll take the baby to the doctor, and I'll call a repairman I know who'll come fix the washing machine right away. Now stop crying. I'll do everything. In fact, I'll even call Joe at work and tell him to come home and help you out."

" Joe?" said Emmy Lou. "Who's Joe?"

"Why, Joe, your husband," said the voice. "Isn't this 225-7318?"

"No," replied Emmy Lou. "This is 225-7381."

"Oh, I'm sorry," said the voice. "I guess I have the wrong number."

There was a moment of silence on the line. "Does this mean you're not coming over?" said Emmy Lou.

Larry was baby-sitting for his younger sister while his parents went to town, and decided to take the girl fishing with him. When his parents returned around suppertime, they found Larry upset.

"I will never take my sister fishing with me ever again. I didn't catch a single fish!"

"Well, don't worry, Larry," his mother replied. "Next time I'm sure she won't cry and scare the fish away."

"It's not that, Ma," said Larry. "She ate all the worms."

Raymond and Cliff were sitting outside the trailer talking about their kids.

"What's your boy going to be when he graduates?" asked Raymond.

"An old man."

Lulu moved out to Hollywood to get discovered and become a famous movie star. Sadly, she found neither fame nor glory. She did find plenty of men, however, who wanted to take advantage of her. One day, she was served with a summons for court. She had been named as the "other woman" in a divorce case.

When it was Lulu's turn to take the stand, the prosecutor stepped toward her. "Miss Lulu Simmons, the defendant's wife has identified you as the "other woman" in her husband's life, and is now suing for divorce. Do you admit that you went to the Shylock Motel with Mr. Samuels?"

"Well, yes," acknowledged Lulu with a sob. "But I couldn't help it!"

"You couldn't help it?" asked the wife's lawyer. "Why couldn't you help it?"

"Because Mr. Samuels deceived me!" she exclaimed.

"Exactly what do you mean, Miss Simmons?" the lawyer asked, with a smile on his face.

"Well, you see," she explained indignantly, "when we signed in, he told the motel clerk that I was his wife!"

DID YOU HEAR ABOUT...

. . . the redneck dog who limped into a bar with one foot all bandaged up? He said, "I wanna see the man who shot my paw!"

. . . the redneck who drove his pickup truck into the lake? His dog drowned while he tried to get the tailgate down.

. . . the disaster in Alabama? There was a terrible power outage at Mobile's largest shopping mall. People were stuck on the escalators for hours.

. . . the redneck who married an Amish woman? He drove her buggy.

. . . the redneck who locked his keys in his car? He had to use a coat hanger to get his family out.

Uncle Jed had a pond on his farm, but there were no ducks in the pond. He had always wanted to have some, so one day he went out and bought a pair. The ducks mated, and within a couple of years, there were ducks everywhere you looked. Jed liked the ducks and didn't have the heart to shoot them, but his farm was fast being overrun. After thinking of all the possibilities, he decided he would give them to the city zoo. He called his nephew, Henry, who had a pickup truck, and said, "Here's ten dollars for you, if you'll take these here ducks to the zoo for me." Henry, who wasn't especially bright, thought for a bit, then agreed. Off he drove with the ducks.

Several hours went by, and Henry had not yet returned from the city. Uncle Jed began to worry that something had gone wrong. He jumped in his car and drove into the city. After driving around for a while, he saw Henry's pickup truck parked outside the local movie theater with his nephew sitting in the cab.

"What happened?" he asked. "Was there any problem with the ducks?"

"Nope," answered Henry, "I still had some money left after taking them to the zoo, though, so I thought I'd take them to the movies."

"Separate that one for beef jerky."

Jesse and J.R. were going elk hunting up north and had hired a plane and a pilot to fly them to the wilderness in northern Canada. The pilot landed on an open field and promised to see them in two days. Their weekend was a resounding success, with the two hunters each bagging four buck. When the plane returned, they began loading their gear and the eight buck on board. But the pilot objected.

"You can't bring back eight elk," he protested. "My plane can only carry six. You'll have to leave two behind."

"But last year we shot eight," replied Jesse, "and the pilot let us put all of them on the plane. And it was the same kind of airplane as you have."

The pilot reluctantly agreed, and the three piled all the elk onto the plane. They closed the door, and the plane rumbled slowly across the meadow before taking off. It wheezed and clunked for a few seconds before plunging to the ground. Shaken but unhurt, the pilot and passengers climbed out of the wreckage and looked around.

"Do you have any idea where we are, J.R.?" asked Jesse.

"I think so," J.R. replied. "It's the same place we crashed last year."

Beauford went to town for his annual medical checkup with Doc Martin. When the doctor finished the exam, he pronounced Beauford fit as a fiddle.

"You're in great shape. Is there anything you'd like to ask me about?"

"Yes, there is, Doc," said Beauford. "I've been thinking about getting one of those vasectomies."

"That's a big decision, Beauford. Have you discussed this with your family?"

"Sure have," replied Beauford. "They're in favor of it, 15 to 2!"

Watty and Homer were discussing their families.

"So, Watty," asked Homer, "just where was your son-in-law when you first saw him?"

"Right in the middle of my shotgun sights," responded Watty.

The tourist stopped his car by the pig farm, and rolled his window down.

"Peeeyou!" he exclaimed, holding his nose. "Hey, mister," he yelled to a farmer leaning against the fence. "Don't you hate the smell of pigs?"

"Well, sir, that depends on the price of pork."

Jack was stretched out beside the lake with his fishing pole propped up next to him with the line dangling in the water. He had a cold beer in his hand and was enjoying the beautiful day, when his solitude was interrupted by an approaching figure. It was a businessman on vacation, carrying expensive gear and outfitted in safari clothes.

"You won't catch many fish that way," said the businessman. "You should be working instead of lying around some lake in west Arkansas."

"What's the reward in that?" asked Jack.

"The reward? Well, you could earn enough to buy a boat and catch more fish."

"What's the reward in that?" Jack inquired again.

"Then you could buy a bigger boat and get people to work for you and catch even more fish."

"So? What's the reward in that?"

The business man was getting exasperated. "Why, you dummy. You could build a fleet of boats and sail around the world and build a fishing empire."

"Where's the reward in that?" Jack persisted.

"Don't you see?" the businessman yelled at Jack . "You'd be so rich, you'd never have to work again. You could spend all your days sitting by a lake, looking at the sunset, not a care in the world."

Jack smiled. "And just what do you think I'm doing right now?"

Lem phoned his wife from the packing plant. "Something just came up, hon," he said. "I've got the opportunity of a lifetime. The guys are going fishing down in the Gulf, and they've got a spot for one more. They're leaving right away. Would you get out my fishing gear and pack my clothes for me? And don't forget my new fancy pajamas."

Lem rushed home, picked up his rods, tackle box, and bag of clothes and threw them in the car. He pecked his wife on the cheek and drove off in a cloud of dust. A week later, he was back.

"Did you have a good time?" his wife sweetly inquired.

"Sure did," said Lem. "It was great being with the guys out on a boat. Forgot all my cares. But one thing, hon. You forgot to pack my pajamas."

"No, Lem, I packed them," she replied. "I stuck them in your tackle box."

"Huey, which is the correct sentence," said the teacher, "'Is the hen laying' or 'Is the hen lying'?"

"It don't really matter, Miss Wilson," Huey replied. "The important thing is she 'laying' or is she 'lying.'"

"Mrs. Jones, it is a shame that your son is illiterate," said the case worker from the Welfare Department.

"He's not illiterate," replied the irate Mrs. Jones. "He was born a week before I was married."

After finishing his morning chores, young Fester walked to school, but was stopped at the door by the principal. "Why, Fester, your hands and face are filthy. Go and wash them this instant. What would you say if I walked into *your* house looking like that?"

"I expect I wouldn't say anything, Mr. Smith," Fester answered. "I'd be too polite to mention it."

A tourist was driving through Mississippi and stopped his car to admire a group of magnificent bulls. He grabbed his camera, got out of the car, and climbed on a fence to get a clearer shot of the animals. While atop his perch, he spied a woman coming out of the barn.

"Hey, lady, are these bulls safe?" yelled the tourist.

The woman looked at him for a moment. "Well, they're a whole lot safer than you are, mister."

Bobby Joe was talking to her ailing 95-year-old mother about the inevitable funeral arrangements that would take place when she died.

"I know you don't want to talk about these things, Ma, but we gotta make some plans about your funeral."

Her mother was silent, so Bobby Joe went on. "For instance, when you die, do you want to be buried or do you want to be cremated?"

The old woman thought for a moment before replying, "I don't rightly know, Bobby Joe. Why don't you just surprise me."

A lost tourist stopped his car at a cabin by the side of the road.

"Hey, Grandpa," the driver yelled to a man rocking on the front porch, "have you lived here all your life?"

The man kept rocking. "Not yet I haven't."

Q: How do you make a redneck laugh on Saturday?

A: Tell him a joke on Wednesday.

The Bible teacher was teaching Sunday School and got into an argument with Patrick.

"And just why do you think that Adam and Eve lived in Arkansas?"

"That's easy, Miss Prewitt. They had no house, no car, no job, and they still thought they were living in Paradise!"

Gaylord and his wife reasoned that the five children they had were quite enough. And so, after much thought, Gaylord decided to get a vasectomy. He drove into town, and stopped at his doctor's office. "Doc, me and the missus don't want to have any more kids, and so I thought I'd get a vasectomy. What do you think?"

"It's a simple procedure, Gaylord, if that's what you've decided," said the doctor. "Takes practically no time at all. In fact, the redneck special is the least expensive and takes just a few seconds."

"Fine. That's the one I want."

The doctor rummaged through a filing cabinet and produced a small hand grenade.

"Here, Gaylord. Take this into the examination room. Remove all your clothes, then sit in the chair. Pull the lever on this grenade, then hold it to your ear, and count to ten."

"Hold it to my ear!" exclaimed Gaylord. "How's that supposed to keep me from having any more kids?"

"Don't worry, Gaylord. Just do as I say."

Gaylord remained unconvinced, but went into the other room to follow the instructions. He undressed and sat in the chair. Then he pulled the lever on the grenade, put it to his ear, and started counting on his right hand. "One, two, three, four, five."

Then he put the grenade between his knees and continued counting on his left hand, "Six, seven, eight. . . . "

"My grandpa is real mad at the county," Loretta said. "They're gonna put a four-lane highway right through his cow pasture."

"Well, why's he mad at that?" asked Conroy. "They're gonna pay him alot of money for it, aren't they?"

"It's not the money; it's the bother. He's afraid that every time a car drives through he's gonna have to run down and open the gate."

"So how come your cousin isn't still driving in the Redneck 500?"

"He kept pulling into the pit to ask directions."

A tourist was driving on a country road in Georgia when he rounded a curve and ran over a hen that was sitting in the middle of the road. He stopped his car, got out, and looked at the flattened fowl. Just then a farmer came out of a nearby barn.

"Hey, mister," the tourist called out. "I'm real sorry, but I just ran over your chicken. Can I give you ten dollars for it?"

"Better make it twenty," the farmer replied. "That was the rooster's only hen and I'm afraid the shock'll kill him, too."

"Hello, long distance operator?" asked Emmy Lou.

"Yes," was the reply.

"I'd like to call my Uncle Ralph in Pascagoula, Mississippi."

"How do you spell that?"

"R A L P H."

"No, the name of the town."

"If I knew how to spell it, I'd write him!"